Practical Guide to the Operational Use of the RPG-7

By Erik Lawrence

Copyright ©2014 Erik Lawrence

Erik Lawrence
www.vig-sec.com   erik@vig-sec.com

Printed and bound in the United States of America

First printing 2006
Second printing 2014

ISBN-10: 1-941998-04-6
ISBN-13: 978-1-941998-04-5
EBOOK – ISBN-13: 978-1-941998-23-6
LCCN: Not yet assigned

ATTENTION US MILITARY UNITS, US GOVERNMENT AGENCIES AND PROFESSIONAL ORGANIZATIONS: Quantity discounts are available on bulk purchases of this book. Special books or book excerpts can also be created to fit specific needs. For information, please contact:

Erik Lawrence
www.vig-sec.com   erik@vig-sec.com

CREDITS:
Wikipedia contributors, "Main Page," Wikipedia, The Free Encyclopedia,
http://en.wikipedia.org/w/index.php?title=Main_Page&oldid=83971314
(accessed October 7, 2006).

Rocket Propelled Grenade Launchers are potentially dangerous and must be handled responsibly by individuals. The technical information presented in this manual on the use of the RPG-7 reflects the author's research, beliefs, and experiences. The information in this book is presented for academic study only. Neither the author nor the publisher assumes any responsibility for the use or misuse of information contained in this book.

SAFETY NOTICE
Before starting an inspection, ensure the weapon is cleared. Do not manipulate the trigger until the weapon has been cleared of all ammunition. Inspect the chamber to ensure that it is empty and no ammunition is present. Keep the weapon oriented in a safe direction when loading and handling.

AMMUNITION NOTICE- these weapons fires multiple types of rockets and they must come from trusted sources, never fire captured rockets. Know the capabilities and limitation of each type of rocket. Firing the incorrect ammunition will damage the weapon and possibly injure the operator/assistant operator.

Training should be received from knowledgeable and experienced operators on this particular weapons system. Vigilant Security Services, LLC provides this training and continually perfects its instruction with up-to-date information from actual use.

www.vig-sec.com

Table of Contents

RPG
Rocket Propelled Grenade Launcher

Section 1

The objective of this manual is to allow the reader to be able to competently use the RPG-7 weapon systems. The manual will give the reader background/specifications of the weapon, instruct on its operation, disassembly and assembly, proper firing procedure, and malfunction/misfire procedures. Operator level maintenance will also be detailed to allow the reader to fully understand and become competent in the use and maintenance of the RPG-7.

Figure 1-1 RPG-7 Light Anti-Tank Rocket Launcher

The RPG-7 are reliable recoilless weapons for destroying tanks, self-propelled artillery units and other armored vehicles of the enemy, as well as the enemy's manpower in open and in armored shelters. This manual was developed to gather, translate and inform users of the basics of the launcher system.

Background

RPG translates to both English Rocket-Propelled Grenade and Russian as *Raketniy Protivotankoviy Granatomet*, "a rocket anti-tank grenade launcher." It was derived through the RPG-2 from the WWII German *Panzerfaust*. The RPG-7 is a recoilless, shoulder-fired, muzzle-loaded, reloadable, antitank grenade launcher. It fires a variety of 85-mm rocket-assisted grenades from a 40-mm smoothbore launcher tube. The launcher has two hand grips, a large optical sight, a wooden heat guard around the middle, and a flared blast shield at the rear of the tube. The launcher is 953 mm long without grenade and 1,340 mm with the rocket. The launcher weighs 7.9 kg and the grenade 2.25 kg. The RPG-7 is light enough to be carried and fired by one person. However, an assistant grenadier normally deploys to the left of the gunner to protect him from small arms fire. The RPG-7 was employed as the standard squad antitank weapon (one per squad) in motorized rifle units and is also found in reconnaissance units.

The internal rocket motor of the PG-7 grenade ignites after traveling 10 meters, giving the projectile higher velocity (sustained out to 500 meters), flatter trajectory, and better accuracy. Accuracy is further enhanced by four large knife-like fins at the rear of the projectile which unfold when the round leaves the tube, and by smaller, offset fins at the very rear, which produce a slow rotation. The maximum effective range is 500 meters for stationary targets and 300 meters for moving targets. Maximum range is 900 meters at which point the projectile self-destructs. The PG-7 grenade, with a shaped-charge warhead, has very good armor penetration (330 mm), capable of defeating all known armored vehicles. The RPG-7V model can be fitted with a telescope and both infrared and passive night sights. All RPG-7 models have an optical sight that can be illuminated for night sighting, and open sights are provided for emergency use.

The RPG-7V requires a well-trained gunner to estimate ranges and lead distances for moving targets. Crosswinds as low as 7 miles per hour can complicate the gunner's estimate and reduce first-round hit probability to 50% at ranges beyond 180 meters. An RPG projectile screen of chain link fence will completely neutralize 50 percent of the rounds and degrade the penetrating capability of the remaining rounds. Reloading and re-aiming the RPG-7 requires a minimum of 14 seconds. Firing leaves noticeable signatures in the form of flash, smoke, and noise, and the unprotected gunner is extremely vulnerable to suppressive fires. In addition to the AT role, it can be used against personnel and for defeating cover. Several countries have developed rounds for RPG-7V.

The grenade launcher is serviced by the gunner and his assistant. The gunner fires the grenade launcher and carriers it with a sling. He also has a carrier containing two rounds, spare parts, tools and accessories

The assistant gunner helps the gunner during delivery of the fire and also carries a carrier with three rounds. When necessary, the assistant gunner replaces the gunner.

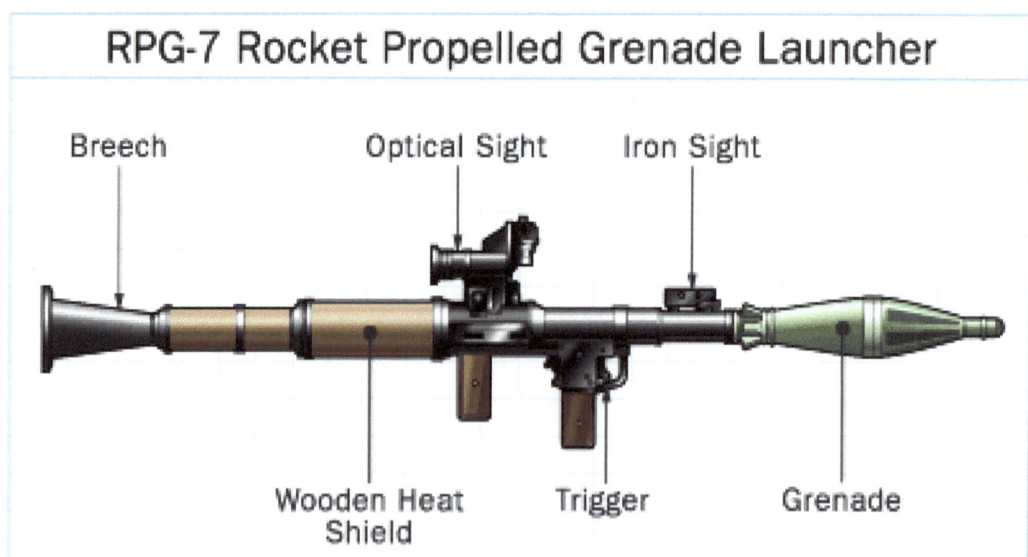

Figure 1-2 Launcher, 40 mm, RPG-7, Light Antitank Grenade

Combat Characteristics

The launcher employs a spigot-type shape-charge grenade. The most effective fire from this grenade launcher is delivered at armored targets at a range of 330 meters. The sighting range of fire is 500 meters. The rate of fire is 4 to 6 rounds per minute.

Characteristics of the Launcher, 40 mm, RPG-7, Light Antitank Grenade (Soviet); Sight, Optical PGO

Caliber of Launcher	40 mm
Caliber of Grenade (as measured at grenade nose) Older round	85 mm
Newer round	70 mm
Length of Launcher	950 mm (37.4 in.)
Length of Grenade without Powder Charge	640 mm (25.2 in.)
Length of Grenade with Powder Charge	925 mm (36.4 in)
Rate of Fire	4-6 rpm
Sighting Range	500 m (547 yds)
Point-blank Range (2 m-high target)	300 m (361 yds)
Weight of Grenade Launcher with Telescopic Sight	6.3 kg (13.9 lbs)
Weight of Round (Grenade with powder charge)	2.25 kg (4.95 lbs)
Weight of Grenade Carrier with Two rounds and Spares, Tools, and Accessories	7.1 kg (15.6 lbs)
Weight of Grenade Carrier with Three Rounds	9.3 kg (20.5 lbs)
Length of Carrier with Grenades	700 mm (27.6 in)
Magnification of Telescopic Sight	2.7 X
Field of Vision	13°
Resolving Power	28 in. max.
Value of Range Scale Graduations	100 m
Value of Deflection Scale Graduations	0-10
Range Scale Limits	200-500 m
Deflection Adjustment Limits in Elevation	0-50
Telescopic Sight Adjustment Limits in Elevation	±0-08
Sight Deflection Adjustment Limits	±0-08
Length of Sight with Eye Shield	140 mm (5.5 in.)
Height of Sight	180 mm (7.1 in.)
Width of Sight	62 mm (2.4 in.)
Weight of Sight	0.5 kg (1.1 lbs)
Weight of Sight with Spares, Tools, Accessories, and Cover	0.95 kg (2.1 lbs)

Launcher Nomenclature

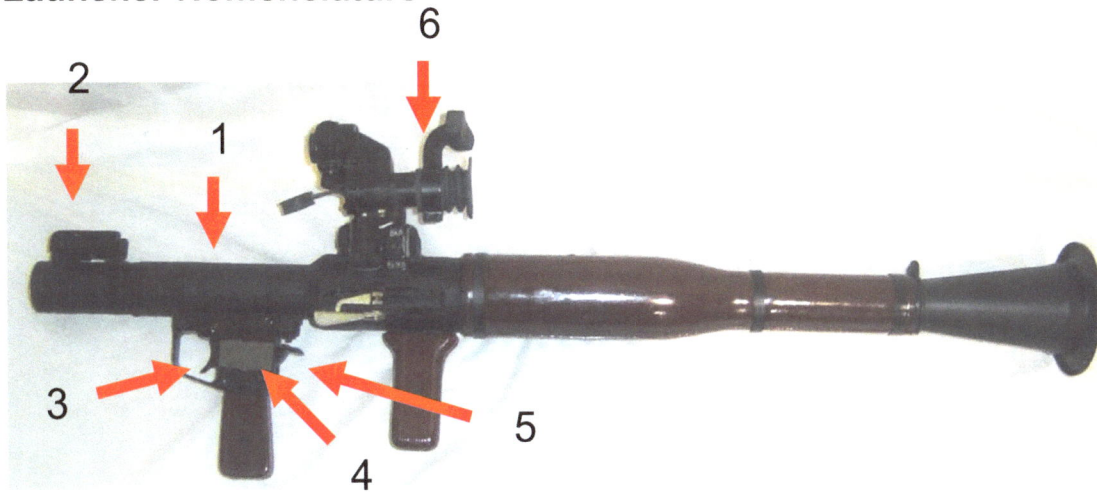

Figure 1-3 Launcher main parts

1. Barrel
2. Open Sight
3. Trigger
4. Safety Lock
5. Striker (hammer)
6. Telescopic Sight

Grenade Nomenclature

Figure 1-4 The rocket assisted grenade consists of the following main parts

1. Nose portion with explosive "warhead"
2. Fuse with safety cap
3. Tab to safety clip to retain safety nose cup
4. Sustainer motor
5. Shipping cap, protects threads
6. Rocket booster and stabilizer (located in the powder charge)
7. Booster plastic shipping tube

Safety When Handling Rounds

- To avoid damage and possible detonation, do not drop the grenades, powder charge, and assemble rounds.
- Carry grenades and their charges in the authorized carriers or packing.
- Protect the grenades and powder charges from moisture, dampness, and direct sunlight.
- Open the case and remove the booster section only before firing. If a grenade prepared for firing is not to be used, unscrew the booster section off the grenade, place it back in the plastic packaging tube to protect the booster thoroughly from damage, moisture, and dampness. Screw the protective cap back onto the rear of the grenade.
- Remove the safety cap from the fuse nose only before loading the grenade launcher. If the grenade has not been fired, fit the safety cap onto the fuse diaphragm for proper restorage.
- Protective caps, safety caps and pins should be kept until after the warhead is fired.
- When firing in rain and hail, do not remove the safety cap from the nose of the fuse. This will prevent premature detonation.
- Keep the grenades and boosters in sub units stored in a cool and dry area, out of direct sunlight to avoid deterioration of the explosives.

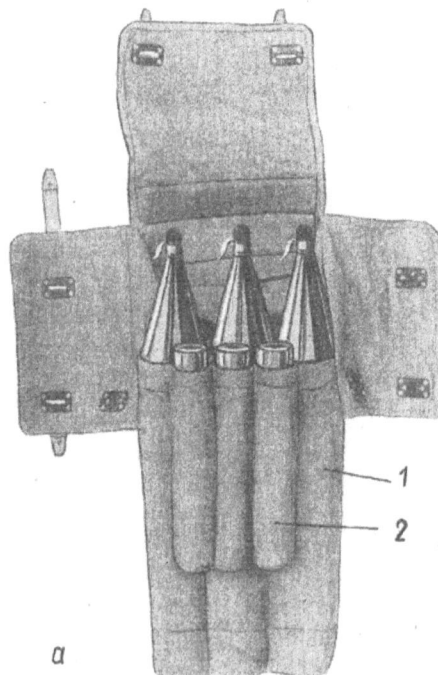

Figure 1-5 Assistant Gunner's Equipment Backpack

1. Rocket
2. Booster

Section 2

Disassembly

The disassembly of the grenade launcher is necessary for cleaning, lubrication and inspection. When attaching or detaching and parts, do not apply excessive force. Do not abruptly strike any part. Use the tools kept in the spare parts, tools, and accessories kit.

Disassembly of the RPG-7

1. Remove the breech and muzzle covers.

2. Use a brass or rubber mallet to tap out the front retaining pin on the pistol grip. Remove the pin and place it to the side.

3. Rotate the pistol grip downward and towards the rear of the launcher. Once the pistol grip is removed from the launcher no further disassembly of the pistol grip is authorized at the operator's maintenance level.

4. Using the wrench provided, remove the firing pin cap by turning it counterclockwise.

5. Lift out the firing pin, firing pin return spring, and firing pin guide. Disassembly is now complete at the operator's maintenance level.

Maintenance

The grenade launcher should be always kept fully serviceable and ready to fire. This is achieved by timely and adequate cleaning, lubrication, and proper storage of the weapon.

Launcher cleaning is performed:

1. After firing practice -- immediately after firing at the range or in the field if time permits. Clean and lubricate both the bore and hammer mechanism. Upon returning from firing practice, clean the launcher again and continue this procedure daily during the next 2 or 3 days.

2. After field exercises without firing – upon returning from the exercise.

3. In combat conditions and during long term training exercises – daily during slow periods in combat/training exercises.

4. When grenade launcher is kept out of operation – once a week.

Launcher Cleaning Procedure

1. To prepare the cleaning rod for cleaning, first remove the front stem of the cleaning rod from the rear stem by pressing on the threaded joint of the front and rear stem of the cleaning rod together as far as they will go (Figure 2-1).

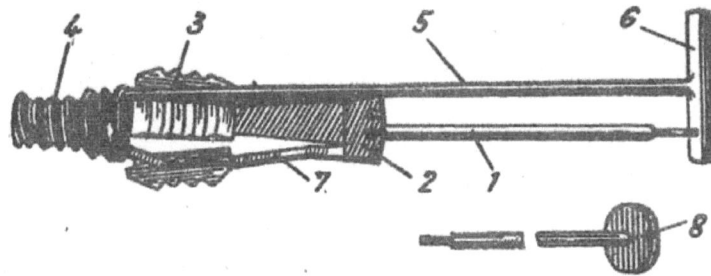

Figure 2-1. Cleaning rod

2. Clean the Bore

   A. Using a thin, soft, lint-free cloth, cover the end face of the cleaning rod scourer. Make sure the cloth evenly covers the scourer and lugs. The cloth should be thin enough to let the cleaning rod enter the bore with a minimum of effort.

   B. Squeeze the cleaning rod lugs and insert the cleaning rod into the muzzle. Clean the muzzle and bore up to the widened end several times until a cloth can be inserted on the scourer and exit without traces of powder or rust.

   C. If you do not have the cleaning rod

      1) Tie a rag to the end of a 5-ft cord, moisten it with bore cleaner, and pull through the launcher. Repeat with clean rags until the weapon is clean. Using the same procedure, lightly oil the bore.

3. Clean the hammer mechanism using a soft cloth and solvent. Wipe the cleaned parts with a dry cloth.

4. Clean the trigger and firing mechanisms with a clean cloth and solvent, wiping dry afterwards.

5. Lubrication

   A. The bore should be oiled with a light coat of L.S.A. to prevent rust. Uses the cleaning rod and attach a soft clean cloth wetted with L.S.A. Run the cloth up and down the bore until an even coat has been deposited. Insure that the entire bore is cleaned and oiled.

   B. All other metal parts should be given a light coat of L.S.A.

   C. In dry sandy climates, the weapon is left un-oiled to prevent sand from accumulating on oiled parts. In this case, the weapon is cleaned more frequently to prevent sand and dirt from interfering with proper operation of the weapon.

   D. Do not lubricate the wooden or plastic parts.

Maintenance of the Telescopic Sight

1. Use lens paper to clean the telescopic lens on the sight.

2. Wipe the external surfaces with a clean cotton cloth. Do not use oil on the sight except on the latching mechanism.

Assembly of the RPG-7

1. Replace the firing pin guide, firing pin return spring, and firing pin.

2. Fasten these parts in place using the firing pin cap by turning it clockwise with the wrench provided until snug.

3. Replace the pistol grip by placing the rear end in first; line up the groove and rotate forward and upward until the holes line up.

4. Replace the front retaining pin using a brass or rubber mallet. The RPG-7 is now ready for use.

Function Check

To perform the function check, place the weapon on safe and pull the trigger. The striker should not fall. If the striker falls, check for worn parts or improper assembly. Next, place the weapon on fire and pull the trigger. If the striker does not fall, check for worn or broken parts or improper assembly.

Use of the Sights

Optical Sight

The PGO-1 is a 2.5X prismatic telescope with a 13° field of view. The reticle has a stadia scale for estimating ranges from 200m to 1000m; the range scale is graduated from 200 m to 500 m (Figure 2-2). Beneath the front lens of the sight is a temperature compensator. This compensator is the knob with a "+" and a "-" sign stamped on the edge. For firing in temperatures above freezing, turn the knob so that the "+" is visible; for below freezing temperatures, turn the knob so that the "-" is visible (Figure 2-3).

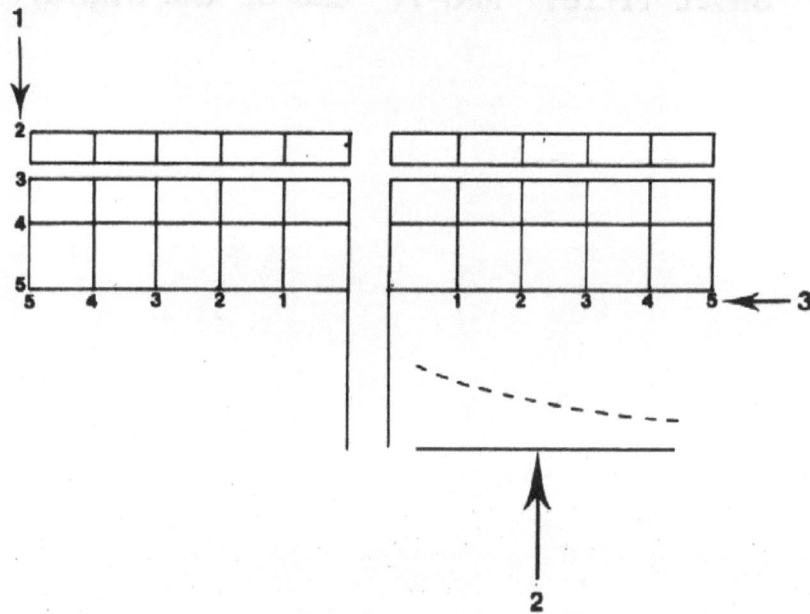

Figure 2-2. Reticle parts

1. Range Scale   2. Stadia Scale   3. Deflection Scale

Practical Guide to the Operational Use of the **RPG-7**

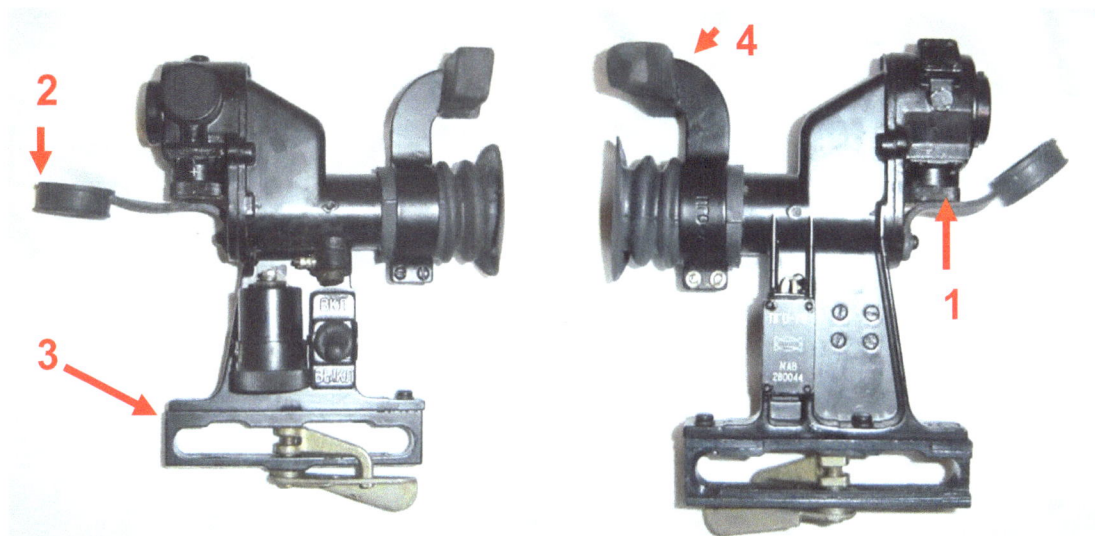

Figure 2-3. PGO-7V optical sight

1. Temperature Compensation Knob
2. Lens Cover
3. Attachment Bracket
4. Forehead Rest

PGO-7V OPTICAL SIGHT FOR THE RPG-7V/TYPE 69 LAUNCHERS

The PGO-7V is a 2.5X prismatic telescope with a 13-degree field of view. A temperature compensator is located under the objective lense. Turn it to "+" or "-," depending on whether the temperature is above or below freezing. The reticle pattern has a stadia scale for estimating ranges from 200 to 1000 meters.

To determine range, you must first set the bottom of the target on the base line, then note the single digit on the stepped scale that aligns with the top of the target. If the actual height of the target is more or less than the scale's given target height, you must take this difference (in tenths of a meter) and multiply it by a constant (four) and the digit on top of the target. This product is then added to, or subtracted from, the range indicated by the stadia scale. All that now remains is for any estimation to be made concerning crosswind deflection. Because of the complicated math required to use this sighting system effectively, it is recommended that iron sights and estimation be used in combat situations.

The Open Sight

1. The open sight is used in cases when the telescopic sight is unserviceable or unavailable. It consists of a sight leaf with slide, primary, and secondary front sights in casings (Figure 2-4).

2. The slide is found on the sight leaf. The slide is moved by depressing in on both sides of the slide catch, which allows the gunner to select the appropriate range (Figure 2-5).

www.vig-sec.com   11

Figure 2-4.   Front and rear sights

Figure 2-5.   Adjusting range on the rear sight

3. The primary front sight is used for firing when temperatures are below freezing (below 0º C or 32º F) (Figure 2-6a).

4. The secondary front sight is used for firing when temperatures are above freezing (above 0º C or 32º F). When it is rotated into the vertical position, it is higher than the primary front sight (Figure 2-6b).

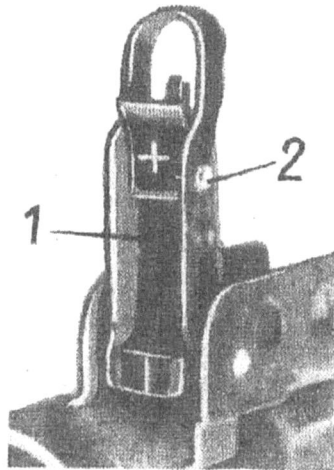 

Figure 2-6 a   Figure 2-6 b
Primary and secondary (lowered) front sights

Selection of Reticle Graduation (Sight Settings) and Aiming Point

1. To select the telescopic sight reticle graduations (open sight settings) and aiming point, it is necessary to determine the range to the target and take into account the conditions that may influence the distance and direction of the grenade flight. When firing at moving targets, it is necessary to consider the direction and speed of the target.

2. The range to the target is determined either by eye or telescopic sight range-finding scale. The knowledge of ranges to ground features (reference points) facilitates the determination of ranges to targets. Therefore, if circumstances allow, the ranges to reference points and ground features should be determined by pacing or by another accurate method.

3. The determination of ranges by eye is carried out by the terrain features well fixed in the visual memory, degree of visibility, and apparent size of targets (objects), as well as by a combination of both methods.

Determining Ranges

1. When determining ranges by the terrain sections, it is necessary to take a range, which is well fixed in your visual memory, for example, a terrain section of 100, 200, 300 or 400 meters and operate with it in measuring mentally the range between you and the target (object). In so doing, the apparent size of the terrain section in the perspective gradually decreases.

2. When determining ranges by the degree of visibility and apparent size of the target (object), it is necessary to compare the visible size of the target with fixed-in mind visible sizes of the target at certain distances.

3. If the target has been discovered near a reference point or ground feature, the range to which is known, then, while determining the range to the target, it is necessary to take into account the distance between the target and reference point.

4. At night, ranges to illuminated targets are determined in the same manner as in daylight. To determine ranges to targets disclosing themselves by muzzle flashes or sounds, it is necessary to multiply the time value estimated in seconds from the moment of flash appearance up to the moment of the second reception by 340 (340 meters per second is the speed of sound).

Ranging Using Telescopic Sight Range-finding Scale

1. To determine ranges by the telescopic sight range-finding scale, the gunner should lay the scale on the target in such a way that the target is between the continuous horizontal line and the curved broken line. The scale touch located above the target indicates the range to the target, with a given target height of 2.7 m. In case the height of the target is less (more) than 2.7 m, it is necessary to subtract (add) a correction, which is equal to the product of tenth of a meter of the target height difference; a constant number 4; and a digit located above the target from the range determined by the scale.

2. Approximately, the correction for the range measured by the scale is taken to be equal to 50 m if the target height deviates from 2.7 m by not more than 0.3 m and 100 m if the target height deviates from 2.7 m by more then 0.3 m.

3. The range to the target may be measured by the range-finding scale only when the full height of the target is seen. If the height of the target is not seen completely, the determination of the range by this scale can lead to gross errors (in this case, the ranges will be, as a rule, increased).

Wind Effects

1. Head winds decrease and trailing winds increase the flight range of the grenade. Weak and moderate winds do not considerably influence the range of the grenade and, hence, no corrections should be introduced for such a wind. If the head wind is strong, aim at the upper edge of the target; if the trailing wind is strong, aim at the lower edge.

2. Side winds exert a considerable effect on the flight of the grenade, blowing it into the wind. For example, if the wind blows from the right, the grenade deviates to the right. If the wind blows from the left, the grenade deviates to the left. This deviation occurs because the side wind blows on the grenade stabilizer, turning the head of the grenade into the wind (Figure 2-7).

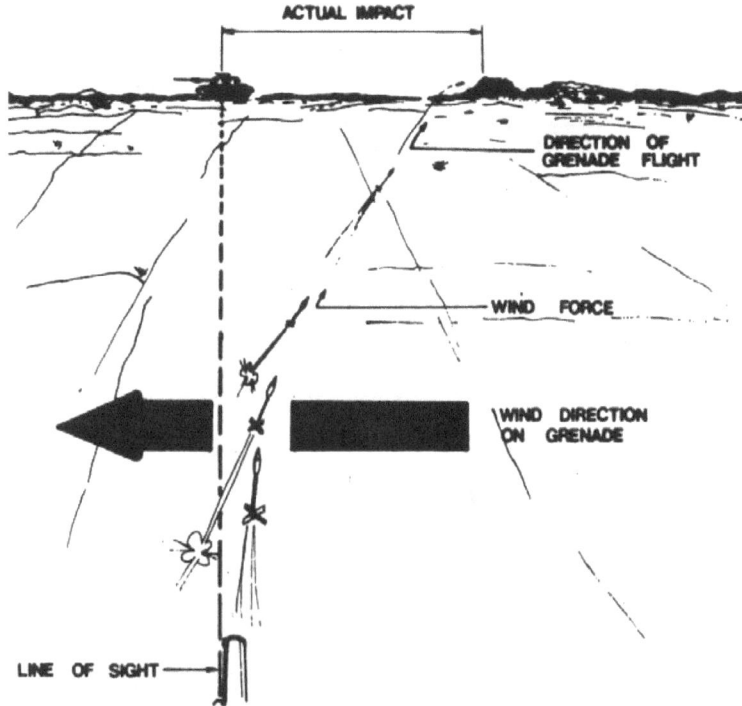

Figure 2-7. RPG-7 round affected by a cross wind.

3. The direction and speed of the wind can be determined empirically.

Estimating Wind Speeds with Visual Clues

- Calm wind - Smoke rises vertically with little if any drift.
- Light Air, 1 to 3 mph - Direction of wind shown by smoke drift, not by wind vanes. Little if any movement with flags. Wind barely moves tree leaves.
- Light Breeze, 4 to 7 mph - Wind felt on face. Leaves rustle and small twigs move. Ordinary wind vanes move.
- Gentle Breeze, 8 to 12 mph - Leaves and small twigs in constant motion. Wind blows up dry leaves from the ground. Flags are extended out.
- Moderate Breeze, 13 to 18 mph - Wind moves small branches. Wind raises dust and loose paper from the ground and drives them along.
- Fresh Breeze, 19 to 24 mph - Large branches and small trees in leaf begin to sway. Crested wavelets form on inland lakes and large rivers.
- Strong Breeze, 25 to 31 mph - Large branches in continuous motion. Whistling sounds heard in overhead or nearby power and telephone lines. Umbrellas used with difficulty.

Wind Notes:

- The correction for a side moderate wind blowing at an angle of 90° to the plane of firing can be taken to be approximately equal to 1.5 graduations of deflection scale for all the ranges of fire of 0.5 silhouette during flank movement and 1 silhouette during frontal movement at ranges up to 300 m and correspondingly 1 and 2 silhouettes at greater distances.

- If a strong wind (8 mps) blows, the corrections given in the table should be doubled and, if a weak wind (2 mps) blows, halved. In this case, the correction for the weak wind should be taken to equal to 0.5 graduations, and the correction for the strong wind to 3 graduations of deflection scale.

- If the wind blows at an acute angle to the plane of firing, the correction should be taken two times less than that for the wind blowing at an angle of 90°.

- When aiming off, take the lead from center of the target.

- When making corrections with the help of the deflection scale, the gunner should choose the aiming point in the center of the target.

Firing at Stationary and Appearing Targets

Firing at stationary and appearing targets should be delivered with the use of the telescopic sight reticle graduations (open sight setting) and aiming point selected in accordance with the range to the target, as well as with the velocity and direction of the side wind.

1. If the range to the target is equal to whole hundreds of meters (for example, 400 m), to aim, the gunner should select the range scale graduation corresponding to this range, i.e., the horizontal line with number 4. When firing with the open sight, the gunner should select sight setting 4 also.

2. While firing against targets at intermediate ranges (for example, 350 m), the gunner should select for an aiming point at the reticle between horizontal lines (in the given example, between lines with numbers 3 and 4).

3. When a side wind blows, the gunner should select for aiming at a stationary target, the point of intersection of the horizontal line, corresponding to the range to the target, and the vertical line, corresponding to the wind correction. When firing with the open sight, the aiming point is set in the target silhouettes to the direction in which the wind blows for side wind correction value.

Firing at Moving Targets

1. For targets directly approaching or moving away from a firing position, the gunner must properly lead the vehicle. He does this by estimating the range to the target at the time of target impact and selecting the telescopic sight reticle graduations and aiming points accordingly. Corrections for side winds must also be taken into account. The correction for side winds is similar to that when engaging stationary targets.

2. When firing at an armored target moving at an angle to the plane of fire, it is necessary to introduce a correction for displacement of the target during the flight of the grenade, as well as to consider the effect of the side wind. The distance covered by the target during flight of the grenade to it is called lead.

   A. While firing the grenade launcher, the lead can be taken in the telescopic sight reticle graduation. In this case, the deflection scale graduations are selected in the part of the reticle from which the target moves. The lead can also be taken in target silhouettes. In this case the central line of the deflection scale (aiming point) is the lead to the direction of the target movement.

   B. The amount of lead depends on the range to the target, its speed, and direction of its movement.

3. The speed of armored targets is determined by eye on the basis of their tactical employment and the nature of terrain. For example, the speed of tanks moving in battle formations of the infantry is 5-6 kHz (1.6 mps); the speed of tanks attacking in cooperation with the infantry in the forward edge of enemy defense equals approximately, 10-12 kph, (3.3 mps), while the average speed of tanks exploiting favorable terrain is 18-20 kph (5 mps) and more.

4. The direction of movement of an armored target relative to the plane of firing is determined by eye based on the relation between the width and length of the target.
   A. If only the hull front (rear) section of the tank (SP gun) is seen, the movement is frontal, i.e., the target moves at an acute angle to the plane of firing.

   B. In case the length of the tank (SP gun) equals, approximately, its width, the movement is oblique, i.e., the target moves at an acute angle to the plane of firing.

C. If the whole length (only the hull side section is seen) of the tank (SP gun) is observed, the movement is flank, i.e., the target moves at an angle of 90° to the plane of firing.

Lead Notes:

- The lead (approx.) for the flank movement of the target with a speed of 15 kph equals 2 deflection scale graduations for all the ranges or 0.5 tank silhouettes for ranges up to 200 m and 1 tank silhouette for greater ranges.

- During an oblique movement of the target (at an acute angle to the plane of firing), the lead should be taken two times less than that during a flank movement.

- The lead in tank silhouettes should be taken from the center of the target.

- If the lead is taken in the deflection scale graduations, select the aiming point in the center of the target.

During flank and oblique movement of the target, the total correction for the lead and the side wind is determined by adding the lead to the wind correction when the direction of the target movement coincides with the wind direction, and by subtracting the side wind correction from the lead when the target moves against the wind. If the difference is positive, consider the lead and, if the difference is negative, take into account the correction for the side wind.

Firing in Poor Visibility Conditions

1. The rules for firing against an illuminated target are the same as for day firing. At the instant the target is illuminated, quickly take aim and fire. To avoid night blindness, do not look directly into the light source.

2. In the case of there is no artificial illumination, aim at the flashes of the tank weapons, the flame from the exhaust pipe, the noise of the engine, or the silhouette of the tank itself.

3. When in mist or smoke, depending on the density of the screen, fire at close ranges at silhouettes or in the direction of engine noise and track clang.

Firing signature

Tests have shown that smoke from the initial firing signature is slightly greater than that of the US M72A2 LAW. The initial booster produces a smoke puff 3 to 4 feet in diameter, which lingers up to 8 seconds in low winds.

Section 3

Operation and Function

Preparing the Grenade (Assistant Gunner)

1. Remove the grenade from the carrying case or the shipping container and inspect the round. Insure that the fuse, nose, nozzle tube of the round, and the powder charge are free of external defects.

Figure 3-1. Warhead and booster inside shipping container

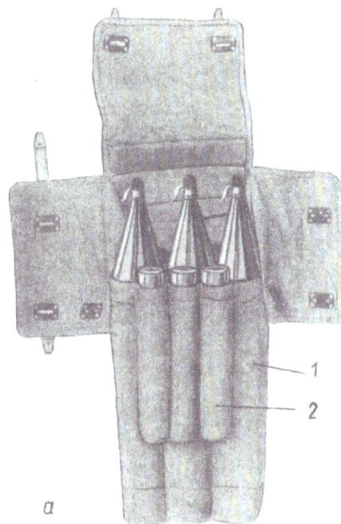

Figure 3-2. Warheads and boosters inside carrying case.

Figure 3-3. Removing nose shipping cap

2. Remove the shipping cap on the nose of the grenade assembly (Figure 3-3).

Figure 3-4. Shipping cap removed from end of grenade assembly

3. Remove the shipping cap from the end of the rocket and grenade assembly (Figure 3-4).

Figure 3-5. Booster element being assembled to the rocket and grenade assembly

4. Assemble the booster element (powder charge) to the rocket and grenade assembly by screwing it clockwise until hand tight (Figures. 3-5 and 3-6).

Figure 3-6. Booster element assembled to the rocket and grenade assembly

5. Only before firing will the assistant gunner remove the safety cap retaining pin from the nose of the grenade by pulling the tape attached to it (Figure 3-7).

WARNING: Because of the sensitivity of the piezoelectric crystal fuse, the cap should not be removed during heavy rain or hail.

Note: Safety caps and pins should be retained until after firing. They must be replaced if the round is prepared but not fired.

Figure 3-7. Removing safety cap retaining pin from grenade

Figure 3-8. Removing safety cap from grenade

6. Remove the safety cap. After loading the prepared round into the prepared launcher and preparing to fire, the safety cap can be removed (Figure 3-8).

Inspecting the Launcher

1. Remove the leather/canvas covers from breech and muzzle, if present.

2. Insure the weapon is on safe. The weapon is safe when the button is pushed through to the right side of the pistol grip (Figure 3-9).

Figure 3-9. Safety button (pushed from left side = SAFE)

3. Inspect the launcher for extraneous matter; look down the bore for obstructions.

4. Raise both front and rear sights unless the optical sight is to be used (Figure 3-10 and 3-11.

Figure 3-10.   Front and rear sights in the raised position

Figure 3-11.   PGO optical sight prior to assembly to RPG-7

Mounting the Optical Sight

1. If the optical sight is to be used, leave the front and rear sights in the down position; place the bottom of the sight along the left side of the RPG-7. Align the groove in the sight with the grooves in the weapon.

2. Slide the PGO sight to its most forward position and secure it using the clamp provided. The sight is now ready for use (Figure 3-12).

Figure 3-12.   PGO-1 optical slid forward and clamped

Loading the Grenade Launcher

CAUTION: Insure the weapon is on SAFE before continuing.

1. Insert the assembled grenade into the launcher muzzle (Figures. 3-13 and 3-14) until the indicator stem, located to the rear of the rocket nozzle moves into the notch in the top edge of the firing pin and primer.

Figure 3-13 Assistant gunner inserting the round

Figure 3-14 Gunner inserting the round

2. If the round fits tightly, load the round by turning it counterclockwise (facing the direction of fire) (Figures 3-15a & b).

Figure 3-15a Aligning the indicator stem with the notch

Figure 3-15b. Indicator stem seated into notched edge of the muzzle

Firing the grenade launcher

Safety - Back blast

1. When preparing the RPG-7 for firing, always check the back blast area. The RPG-7 is almost as dangerous to the rear as it is to the front. Propellant gases from the rear of the RPG-7 create a back blast area 45 meters deep and 25 meters wide at the base. This back blast area consists of two smaller areas:

   A. The danger area is 20 meters to the rear, 8 meters at the base. All personnel, equipment and flammable materials must be cleared from this area.

   B. The caution area is 25 meters beyond the danger area with a 25 meter base.

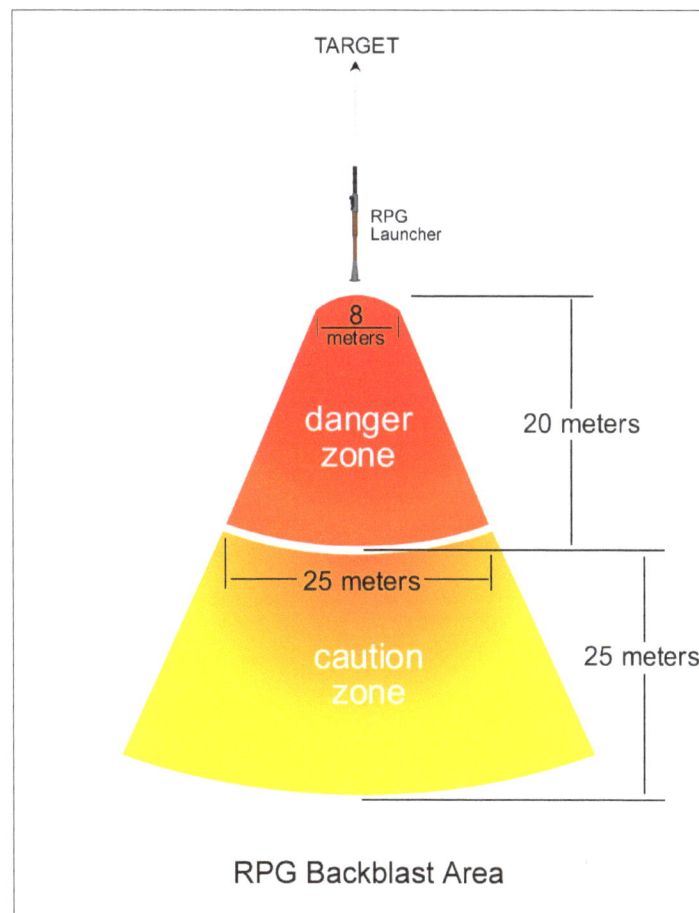

TARGET

RPG Launcher

8 meters

danger zone

20 meters

25 meters

caution zone

25 meters

RPG Backblast Area

2. During training, both areas must be clear of personnel and equipment; during combat, the caution area may be omitted as long as personnel in the area are forewarned.

Firing Sequence

The first step to employing the RPG 7 is to find the best available firing position. Some of the factors which determine position selection are the amount of cover and concealment and very importantly, a properly cleared back-blast area. The area to the rear of the firing position must be cleared of all personnel and equipment for 20 meters. Additionally if possible debris must be removed to prevent secondary missile hazards. This step will also reduce the chance of detection of the position because of all the debris being blown around.

Proper firing requires the following operations: Sight setting, positioning, aiming, cocking, hammer release, and steadying the weapon.

Setting the Sight

a. To set the rear open sight, depress the slide catch and move the sight slide along the sight leaf until the lower face of the opening matches with the desired mark (estimated range) on the sight leaf.

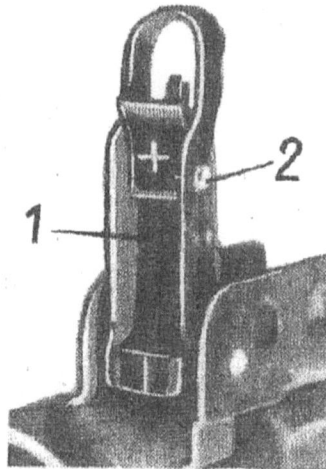

Figure 3-16. Primary front sight

1. When firing the weapon in temperatures below freezing (0° C or 32° F), use the primary front sight, marked with the "+" (Figure 3-16).

Figure 3-17. Secondary front sight

2. When firing the weapon in temperatures above freezing (0° C or 32° F), use the secondary front sight. When it is rotated into the vertical position, it is higher than the primary front sight (Figure 3-17).

3. When using the telescopic optical sight, install it as indicated in the launcher preparation section as previous detailed. When using the optical sight, the metal sights remain in the lowered position.

Proper Positions

The following positions are used when firing the RPG-7:

1. Prone Position (Figure 3-18) – used when there is little cover or concealment. It provides a low profile for the gunner and the assistant gunner and therefore the most protection. This allows quick movement for either the gunner or assistant gunner. The prone position also may not afford the gunner a good view over the battlefield. To fire, rest the elbows on the ground in the most convenient manner approximately a shoulder width apart, with the body approximately 45° to the line of the launcher. This position will allow the gunner to avoid the back blast.

Figure 3-18. Prone position

2. Kneeling Position (Figure 3-19) – used when there is cover available. This position provides the gunner a stabilized position and affords him the capability to move quickly after a round has been fired. The kneeling position exposes the gunner and assistant gunner if adequate cover is not used. To fire from this position, rest the left elbow against the thigh of the left leg or around the left knee. The right elbow is pushed into the body to stabilize the weapon.

Figure 3-19. Kneeling position

3. Standing Position (Figure 3-20) – the standing position is used when forward movement demands quick fire and movement tactics. This position should be used with cover wherever possible since it provides a high-visibility profile. Very little support exists for the weapon in this position. To fire, keep the elbows pressed in close to the body and keep the feet about a shoulder width apart, with the left foot in front of the right for support.

Figure 3-20. Standing position

The following steps should be followed with all three firing positions:

1. Place the barrel on the right shoulder and hold it by the barrel grip with the non dominant hand. With the dominant hand, grasp the firing and trigger mechanism. The weapon system is designed to be fired on the right shoulder. Hand positions may be altered to the preference of the firer.

2. Point the grenade towards the target.

3. Cock the hammer (Figure 3-21) by applying a downward pressure with either the thumb or forefinger.

4. Place the weapon off safe (Figure 3-22).

5. Put the forefinger of the forward hand on the trigger.

6. Press the right cheek against the wooden hand guard.

Figure 3-21. Cocking the hammer

Figure 3-22. Weapon off safe ready to fire (pushed from right = FIRE)

Taking Aim

Note: Because of the flight characteristics of the RPG-7 grenade, wind and weather factors need be considered when aiming the weapons.

When firing with the telescopic sight, close the left eye, and with the right eye pressed against the eye shield, look through the eyepiece to the target. Determine the range up to the target with the help of the range finding scale. Aim the sight reticle at the target. with the horizontal line corresponding to the range to the target (sight setting) and vertical line corresponding to the lateral correction. Make sight corrections by moving the elbows and the body rather than canting the weapon (Figure 3-23).

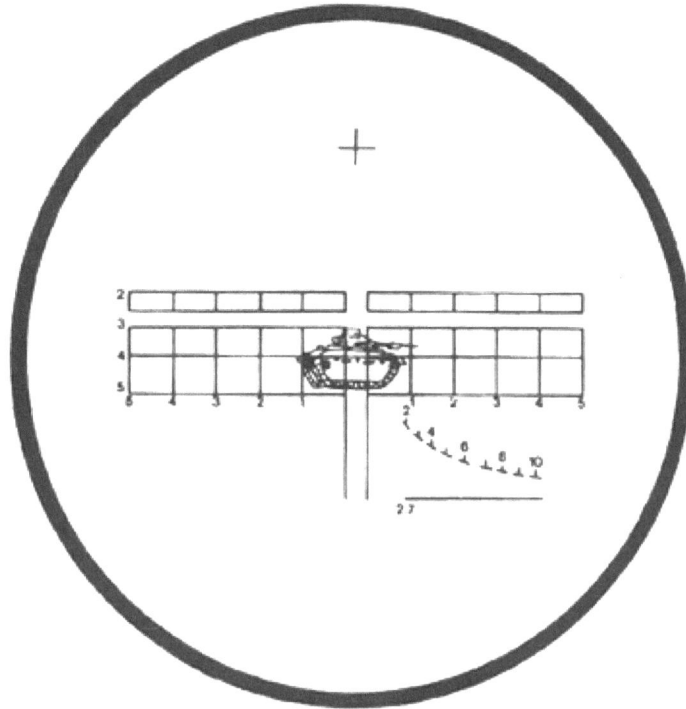

Figure 3-23. Aiming when firing the launcher with telescopic sight against a tank at a range of 400 m (no lateral correction)

When firing with the open sight, close the left eye, and with the right eye, look through the slide notch at the front sight tip so that the front sight is in the middle of the notch and its tip is on the level with the upper edges of the notch, i.e., to obtain the normal sight and align it on the aiming point (Figure 3-24).

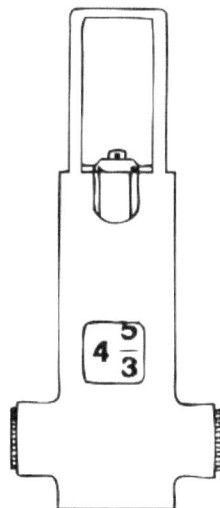

Figure 3-24. Aiming with open sights at a range of 400 meters

Releasing the Hammer

To release the hammer hold your breath and squeeze the trigger gradually until the shot is fired.

Holding the Grenade Launcher During Fire

Because of the design of the weapon, there is no recoil when firing the RPG-7. The gunner should hold the weapon firmly when aiming and throughout the firing sequence. The gunner should not flinch or jerk at the trigger. This action may cause the launcher to move away from the proper aiming point. After firing the grenade, keep the launcher aimed at the target. Second shot point-of-aim may have to be adjusted by noting the grenade burst with relation to the sight picture.

Cease Fire Procedures

If it becomes necessary to cease fire, the following steps should be followed:

1. Gunner - Finger off the trigger.
2. Gunner - Set the launcher on safe.
3. Assistant Gunner - Remove the grenade from the launcher.
4. Assistant Gunner - Replace the safety cap on the fuse head section and secure it with the safety cap retaining pin.
5. Gunner - Release the hammer by holding the hammer with the right thumb, pull the trigger with the forefinger, and allow the hammer to go upward slowly and controlled.
6. Assistant Gunner - Unscrew the booster charge from the grenade and replace it in the container or carrying bag.
7. Gunner - Replace the muzzle and breech covers.
8. Assistant Gunner - Screw the protective cap onto the rocket bottom.
9. Gunner - Replace the lens cover on the telescopic lens and remove the optical sight.

Note: If the gunner is alone, he first removes the round, services the launcher, and finally the round.

Tactics History of the RPG

RPGs are a low-cost, low-tech, direct fire man-portable weapon, used primarily to engage thinly-armored and unarmored vehicles and personnel. It also can be used as an anti-aircraft weapon, usually against helicopters.

Because of the inherent inaccuracy of the RPG, the operator must fire relatively close to the intended target, increasing the chances of being spotted and suppressed. Most modern armies use the ATGM as their primary infantry anti-tank weapon, but the RPG can still be used effectively under certain tactical conditions, especially urban warfare, where they are favored by low-tech armies and terrorist organizations. They are most effective when used in restricted terrain, as the availability of cover and concealment can make it difficult for the intended target to spot the RPG operator before moving into his kill zone.

The operator must move after firing the RPG as the ignition of the rocket generates a flash visible to the enemy and usually leaves a smoke trail leading back to the firing position. In Afghanistan, Mujahadeen RPG shooters who remained in position after firing were often killed by Soviet counter-fire.

In Afghanistan, Mujahadeen guerrillas used RPG-7s to destroy invading Soviet vehicles. To assure a kill, two to four RPG shooters would be assigned to each vehicle. In areas where vehicles were confined to a single path (a mountain road, swamps, snow, urban areas), RPG teams trapped convoys by destroying the first and last vehicles in line, preventing movement of the other vehicles. This tactic was especially effective in cities. Convoys learned to avoid approaches with overhangs and to send infantrymen forward as a screen in hazardous areas.

Multiple shooters were also effective against heavy tanks with reactive armor. The first shot would be against the driver's viewing prisms. Following shots would be in pairs, one to set off the reactive armor, the second to penetrate the tank's armor. Favored weak spots were the top and rear of the turret. Chechen guerillas also attacked Russian tanks from basements, effective because the tanks' guns could not depress far enough to return fire. Both artillery suppression and infantry screens prevented antitank attacks by RPG teams. Russian tank columns were eventually protected by attached mobile anti-aircraft artillery used in the ground role to suppress and destroy Chechen ambushes.

South African and Soviet armored personnel carriers (APC) would be targeted as soon as they stopped to let off troops. The South Africans developed a doctrine of driving the APC in widening circles, using automatic gunfire from one side to destroy the RPG teams. This prevented the APCs from becoming stationary targets as they would if they stopped to let off troops.

The RPG is somewhat useful in the anti-aircraft role. Helicopters would typically be ambushed as they landed or hovered. Again, multiple launchers were needed in order to increase the chances of a hit. Both of the Blackhawk helicopters lost by the U.S. in Mogadishu, Somalia, were downed by RPG-7s. In Afghanistan, Soviet helicopters countered by clearing landing zones (LZ) with anti-personnel saturation fire. They also began arriving with unpredictable numbers of wingmen (two or three), to upset Afghan force estimations and preparation. The Afghans countered by digging prepared firing positions with top cover. The Soviets countered this by using air-dropped fuel-air bombs to clear LZs. The Afghans were able to counter this by using U.S.-supplied Stinger surface-to-air missiles and finally prevailed.

Afghans sometimes used RPG-7s at extreme long range, exploded by their 4.5 second self-destructs, which calculates to an almost 1 km range. This approach performed expedient indirect anti-personnel bombardment and was sometimes used to discourage reconnaissance by aircraft.

Section 4

Misfire Procedure

In the event of a misfire, extreme care and caution must be exercised with the RPG-7. If the hammer strikes the firing pin and the booster does not ignite, make certain the round is aligned and properly seated in the launcher. Re-cock the weapon and attempt to fire again. If the weapon still does not fire, keep the weapon pointed down range, clear the range, and wait five minutes. After five (5) minutes, the assistant gunner or safety officer/NCO will carefully remove the round from the launcher. He will inspect the misfired round to make certain that the primer has been struck. If so, the fault is probably in the round and it should be placed in the misfire/dud pit. In this case, call the nearest E.O.D. unit to dispose of the round. If the primer has been improperly struck or not struck at all, send the launcher in for repair and fire the round from another launcher.

Troubleshooting

The following chart may be used to assist the gunner in determining the cause of an improperly fired round:

Issue	Cause	Remedy
Misfire	1. Round not properly loaded into launcher	1. Reload the round, insuring that the grenade is properly seated in the launcher with the indicator stem seated in the notch.
	2. Grenade primer defective	2. Replace grenade.
	3. Hammer worn or broken	3. Replace hammer.
	4. Sluggish hit of hammer against primer	4. Clean firing pin, hammer trigger, and hammer mechanism.
Rounds fail to enter bore.	1. Dirty bore	1. Clean bore.
Rounds fall once boosted from launcher.	1. Second stage on grenade is faulty.	1. Replace all grenades and boosters.

Appendix A- Ammunition for RPG

The following pictures show ammunition in various stages of packing and assembly.

Figure A-1 The rocket-assisted grenade consists of the following main parts:

1. Nose portion with explosive "warhead"
2. Fuse covered by safety cap
3. Tab to safety clip to retain safety nose cap
4. Sustainer motor

5. Shipping cap, protects threads
6. Rocket booster and stabilizer (located in the powder charge)
7. Booster plastic shipping tube

Figure A-2. Warhead and booster inside shipping container

Figure A-3 Grenade assembly in packaging

Figure A-4 Booster assembly in packaging

Note: Fin assembly is encased in cardboard which burns off when the booster ignites and the round clears the muzzle of the RPG-7. Pieces of this cardboard can remain in the launcher bore and cause obstructions.

Figure A-5. Warhead and booster element/fin assembly assembled.

Figure A-6. RPG-7 85 mm projectile (top) and
RPG-7M 70 mm projectile (bottom)

Warheads

The High Explosive (HE) warhead (grenade) is a general-purpose explosive warhead for use against unarmored targets such as infantry, unarmored wheeled vehicles, and fixed positions. The HE warhead detonates upon impact. The warhead case and charge generate moderate amounts of shrapnel.

The HEAT (anti-tank) round is a standard shaped-charge warhead, similar in concept to those used in tank cannon rounds. In this type of warhead, the shape of the explosive material within the warhead focuses the explosive energy on a copper (or similar metal) lining. This crushes the metal lining and propels some of it forward at a very high velocity. The resulting narrow jet of metal can punch through Rolled Homogenous Armor (RHA) used in many armored vehicles, including some types of main battle tanks. Although the warhead on RPG systems is too small to penetrate the main armor of most modern battle tanks, it is still capable of secondary damage to vulnerable systems (especially sights, tracks, rear and roof of turrets) and can also penetrate most lightly armored or unarmored vehicles.

Specialized warheads are available for illumination, smoke, tear gas, and white phosphorus. Russia, China, and many former Warsaw Pact nations have also developed a fuel-air explosive warhead. Another recent development is a tandem HEAT warhead capable of penetrating reactive armor.

Accuracy limits the standard RPG-7 to a practical range of 50 m, although it can reach 150 or even 300 m in skilled hands. It has an indirect fire (bombardment) range to 920 m, limited by the 4.5 second self-destruct timer.

The High Explosive Anti Tank (HEAT) warhead comes in two sizes: 85 mm and the newer round, 70 mm (Figure 6-7). An inert grenade with a black warhead is used for practice; however, the rocket motor is painted olive drab to indicate that it is alive. The grenade consists of three main sections: warhead, rocket motor, and tail assembly. The warhead has a point-initiating, base-detonating fuse with a piezoelectric crystal element in the nose. This element is crushed when it strikes an object, generating electric current to the base detonating fuse.

Rocket Types

The RPG-7 can fire a variety of warheads for anti-armor (HEAT, PG-) or anti-personnel (HE, OG-) purposes, usually fitting with an impact (PIBD) and a 4.5 second fuse. Armor penetration is warhead dependent and ranges from 30 to 60 cm of homogenous steel; two warhead types (PG-7BR and VR) are 'tandem' devices, used to defeat reactive armor with a single shot. Six rounds in a wooden case, 6 grenades packed separated from 6 booster charges. Dimensions of case, 798mm x 452mm x 245mm/31.5" x 17.8" x 9.6", weight is 33kg/73 pounds.

Prior to the use, the ammunition must be inspected for serviceability. To begin, first inspect the round to insure that it is not dented in any way. If the round is dented, it must discarded, as it is unserviceable. If the propellant charge is dirty, it must be cleaned prior to use. If the charge is dented it is still serviceable provided that the cardboard is not cut, broken, or wet. If both components are determined serviceable, they are connected by simply screwing them together. Now remove the safety cap just prior to loading the complete projectile into the launcher.

Current production ammunition for the RPG-7V1 consists of three types:

- **PG-7VL** standard HEAT warhead for most vehicle and fortification targets
- **PG-7VR** dual HEAT warhead for defeating modern heavily armored vehicles
- **TBG-7V** thermobaric warhead for anti-personnel and urban warfare
- **Caliber:** 40 mm/1.57 inches
- **Weight:** 7 kg/15 pounds
- **Length:** 95 cm/37 inches
- **PG-7VL:**
  - **Warhead:** Single-stage high explosive anti-tank
  - **Round weight:** 2.6 kg/5.7 pounds
  - **Diameter:** 93 mm/3.65 inches
  - **Penetration:** 60 cm/24 inches
- **PG-7VR:**
  - **Warhead:** Tandem high explosive anti-tank
  - **Round weight:** 4.5 kg/9.9 pounds
  - **Diameter:** 10.5 cm/4.1 inches
  - **Penetration:** 75 cm RHA after reactive armor/30 inches
- **TBG-7V:**
  - **Warhead:** Single-stage thermobaric
  - **Round weight:** 4.5 kg/9.9 pounds
  - **Diameter:** 10.5 cm/4.1 inches
  - **Kill radius:** 8 m/26 feet

Ammunition Operational Characteristics

1. When the grenade launcher is fired, the hammer hits the firing pin, which strikes the primer, and the power charge ignites. Gases produced by the burning powder propel the grenade from the grenade launcher.

2. After the grenade has cleared the launcher bore, the stabilizer fins open and the fuse is armed. The powder charge of the rocket booster ignites

approximately 11 meters from the launcher and produces a bright flash and a second puff of smoke similar to the initial blast (Figure 6-1).

3. Upon impact of the grenade with an obstacle (target), the fuse operates and the bursting charge explodes, thereby generating an armor-piercing (concentrated, directed) jet.

4. The grenade launcher does not recoil when fired since the gases rush backward through the muzzle and bell-mouth of the launcher.

5. If a target is not hit, the round will self-destruct approximately 920 meters down range.

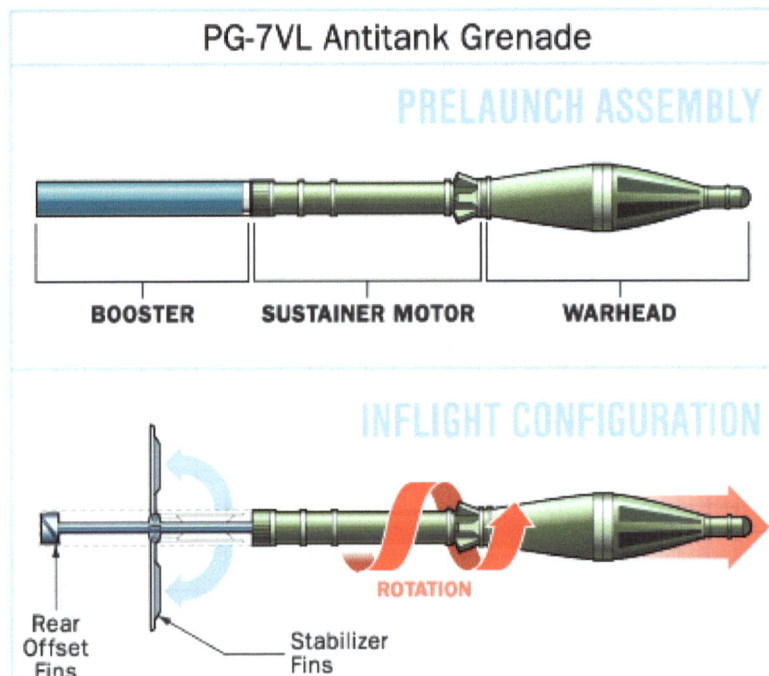

Figure A-7. Grenade flight characteristics.

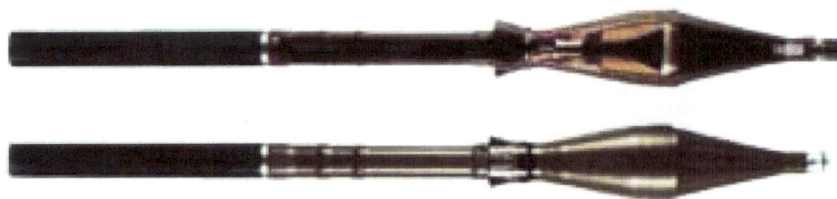

Figure A-8. PG-7V Hollow-charge Round

It is intended for destroying tanks, self-propelled guns, and other armored vehicles. It can also be used against enemy troops in field shelters and in different fortifications. It is equipped with the VP-7M fuse.

Figure A-9. PG-7VN Hollow-charge Round

It is designed for destroying tanks, self-propelled guns and other armored vehicles. It can also be used against enemy troops in field shelters and in different fortifications. It is equipped with the VP-22 fuse.

Figure A-10. PG-7VM Hollow-Charge Round

It is designed for destroying tanks, self-propelled guns, and other armored vehicles. It can also be used against enemy troops in field shelters and in different fortifications. It is equipped with the VP-7M fuse.

Figure A-11. PG-7VLT Hollow-charge round with PG-7LT
tandem anti-tank grenade

Intended for destroying tanks (including those with explosive resistant armor - ERA), self-propelled guns, and other armored vehicles. It can also be used suppressing infantry and firing posts in brick and reinforced concrete buildings and log-and-earth shelters.

Figure A-12. OG-7V Round with OG-7 Fragmentation grenade

It is designed for destroying the enemy troops in the open, in trenches, field shelters, and different fortifications. It is equipped with the O-4M fuse.

Figure A-13. OG-7VM High-explosive round

It is designed for destroying the enemy troops in the open, in trenches, in field shelters or different fortifications. It is equipped with the O-4M fuse.

Figure A-14. OG-7VMZ High-explosive Round

It is designed for destroying the enemy troops in the open, in trenches, in field shelters, or different fortifications, as well as for destroying light armored and unarmored vehicles. The warhead contains powerful explosive and prefabricated fragments, increasing its fragmentation effect. It is equipped with the O-4M impact fuse. The design enables the usage of delay and proximity fuses.

Figure A-15. OG-7VE High-explosive Round

It is intended for destroying the enemy troops in the open, in trenches, and in hasty field shelters, as well as against hostile unarmored motorized and mechanized vehicles. The grenade is equipped with a warhead containing pre-fragmented steel rings and bursting charge of explosive or explosive mixture of powerful high-explosive incendiary action. The round is completed with the GO-2 impact fuse and propelling charge of strip ballistic powder.

Figure A-16. KO-7V Round with KO-7 Hollow-charge Fragmentation Grenade

It is intended for the destruction of tanks, self-propelled guns, and other armored and motorized and mechanized vehicles, as well as for destroying the enemy manpower in the open, in trenches, light field shelters, and brick fortifications of the urban type. The grenade warhead is a combination of a bursting fragmentation hollow charge and pre-fragmented steel rings. The warhead is completed with the

VP-22M nose-base piezoelectric fuse with an inertial self-destroyer for firing at a distance up to 2000 m.

Figure A-17. GTB-7VS Thermobaric Round

Intended for destroying the enemy emplacements (battlefield fortifications, reinforced buildings, stone, brick or concrete fortifications), light armored vehicles and automobiles, and enemy troops in the open and in shelters.

Rules for Handling Rounds

1. To avoid damage and possible detonation, do not drop the grenade, powder charge, and assembled rounds.

2. Carry grenades and their charges in the authorized carriers or packing.

3. Protect the grenades and powder charges from moisture, dampness, and direct sun.

4. Open the case and remove the powder charge only before firing. If a grenade prepared for firing is not to be used, screw the powder charge off the grenade, place it into the packing case, and thoroughly protect the powder charge from damage, moisture, and dampness. Screw the protective cap onto the rocket bottom.

5. Remove the safety cap from the fuse nose only before loading the grenade launcher. If the grenade has not been fired, fit the safety cap onto the fuse diaphragm for proper restorage.

6. Protective caps, safety caps, and pins should be kept until after the warhead is fired.

7. When firing in rain and hail, do not remove the safety cap from the nose of the fuse. This step will prevent premature detonation.

8. Keep the grenades and powder charges in sub units stored in a cool dry area, out of direct sunlight to avoid deterioration of the explosive.

Appendix B- Boresighting the Launcher

In order to engage targets effectively with the RPG 7, the weapon must be boresighted. Boresighting aligns the bore of the weapon with the sight.

To boresight the RPG 7, you must first clear the weapon. Then the weapon must be secured so that it is stable. This can be done with sandbags. Secure two pieces of thread to the boresight gauge with tape or rubber bands, which forms a crosshair centered in the center of the gauge. Next place the gauge into the muzzle of the launcher. The gauge has a stud, which must be aligned with the slot on the muzzle of the launcher. Position the launcher so that the crosshairs are centered on a distant aiming point more than 300 meters from the weapon. Now look through the sight. The '+' in the upper part of the telescope should be aligned with the aiming point. If it is not, you must adjust the sight. To do this, you unscrew the cover of the lateral adjustment screw. Insert a screwdriver blade into the slit of the screw and rotate until the '+' is aligned with the vertical plane of the distant aiming point. Then loosen the three side screws provided on the temperature correction knob 1 1/2 to 2 revolutions. Rotate the elevation adjustment screw, located in the center, until the '+' is on the same point as the crosshairs of the boresight gauge. Finally, recheck the crosshairs of the boresight gauge against the sight picture. If they are aligned, the boresighting is complete. If not, repeat the procedure. Retighten the three screws and replace the cover on the lateral adjustment screw. If you have boresighted the weapon properly, you can be assured that it will hit where you aim it.

Appendix C - Ammunition Comparison

9x18mm
Makarov

9x19mm
Luger

7.62x25mm
Tokarev

.45 ACP

PISTOLS AND SUBMACHINE GUNS

Size Comparison of NATO vs. Non-Standard Ammunition

5.56x
45mm

5.45x
39mm

5.56x
45mm

7.62x
39mm

7.62x
51mm

7.62x
54R mm

12.7x
99mm

12.7x
108mm

ASSAULT RIFLES

SNIPER RIFLES & MACHINE GUNS

Appendix D - Non-Standard Ammunition Packaging & Markings

Packaging

Russian small arms cartridges are packed in sealed sheet-metal containers, with two containers per wooden crate. Older Russian production used rectangular containers of heavy gauge galvanized iron with soldered seams. Around 1959, the introduction of painted, rolled edge, rounded corner, tin plate 'sardine can' containers became the standard.

Metal and wooden crates have standardized markings that identify the contents as to caliber, functional type, cartridge case material, quantity and cartridge/powder lot data. Specialized cartridges are further identified by a color code consisting of one or two color stripes which correspond to bullet tip color. AP cartridges with tungsten carbide cores are identified by two concentric circles instead of color stripes. Russian cartridge designation, packaging and marking practices are generally followed by former Soviet-Bloc countries; each, however, has introduced some modifications in designation and marking. Russian ammunition packaging can be distinguished from Bulgarian packaging, which also carries Cyrillic markings, primarily by the different factory codes. The factory code on the container also appears in the headstamp of the cartridges in the container.

Steel Ammo Tins
(Sardine Cans)

Wood Ammo Crate (Case)
(Contains 2 Tins + Opener)

Cartridge quantities and weights of wooden crates

Country	Manufacturer	Caliber	Rounds /Crate	Crate Weight
Czech Rep.	Sellier and Bellot	14.5 x 114	210	53 kg.
India	OFB	14.5 x 114	60	15.5 kg.
Russia	Unknown	14.5 x 114	80	23 kg.
Bulgaria	Arsenal	12.7 x 108	200	29 kg.
Bulgaria	Arsenal	12.7 x 108	200	32 kg.
Pakistan	POF	12.7 x 108	280	42 kg.
Russia	Unknown	12.7 x 108	190	29 kg.
Russia	Novosibirsk	12.7 x 108	160	25 kg.
Bulgaria	Arsenal	7.62 x 54(R)	880	25 kg.
Czech Rep.	Sellier and Bellot	7.62 x 54(R)	800	24 kg.
Russia	Novosibirsk	7.62 x 54(R)	880	26 kg.
Russia	Novosibirsk	7.62 x 54(R)	600	21 kg.
Russia	Unknown	7.62 x 54(R)	880	26 kg.
Serbia	Prvi Partizan	7.62 x 54(R)	1,200	39 kg.
Czech Rep.	Sellier and Bellot	7.62 x 39	1,200	28 kg.
Pakistan	POF	7.62 x 39	1,750	39 kg.
Russia	Barnaul	7.62 x 39	1,320	30 kg.
Serbia	Prvi Partizan	7.62 x 39	1,260	29 kg.
Sudan	STC	7.62 x 39	1,500	28.1 kg.
Ukraine	Lugansk	7.62 x 39	1,320	30 kg.
Yugoslavia	Igman Zavod	7.62 x 39	1,260	28 kg.
Yugoslavia	Igman Zavod	7.62 x 39	1,120	27.5 kg.
Russia	Unknown	5.45 x 39	2,160	29 kg.
Ukraine	Lugansk	5.45 x 39	2,160	29 kg.

Non-Standard Ammunition tin and crate marking - diagrams

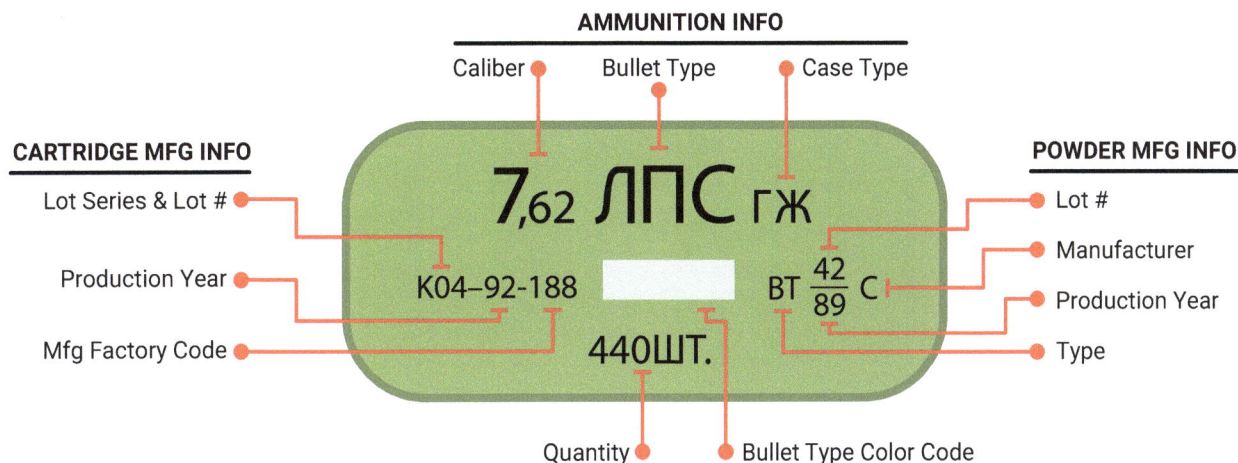

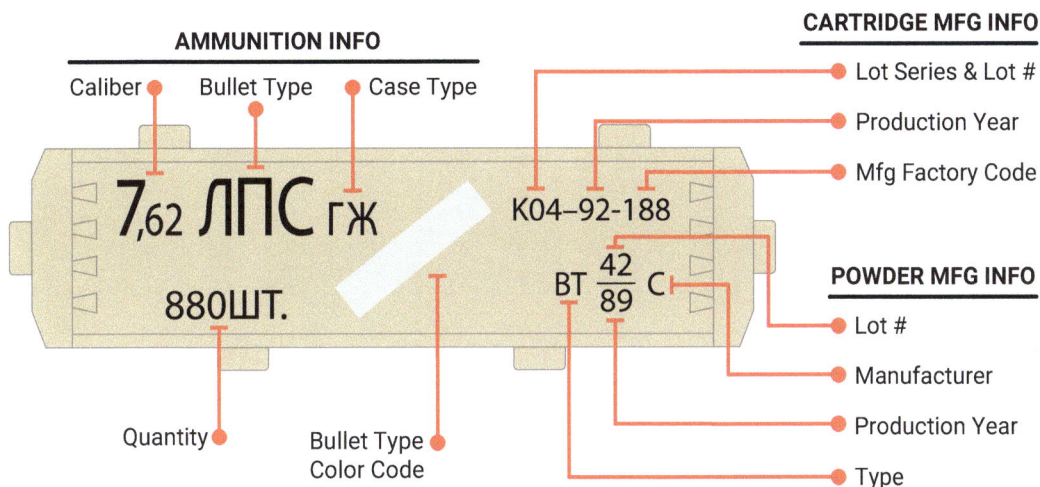

AMMUNITION INFO

Caliber   Bullet Type   Case Type

CARTRIDGE MFG INFO

Lot Series & Lot #

Production Year

Mfg Factory Code

7,62 ЛПС ГЖ

K04–92–188

440ШТ.

BT $\frac{42}{89}$ C

POWDER MFG INFO

Lot #

Manufacturer

Production Year

Type

Quantity   Bullet Type Color Code

AMMUNITION INFO

Caliber   Bullet Type   Case Type

CARTRIDGE MFG INFO

Lot Series & Lot #

Production Year

Mfg Factory Code

7,62 ЛПС ГЖ

880ШТ.

K04–92–188

BT $\frac{42}{89}$ C

POWDER MFG INFO

Lot #

Manufacturer

Production Year

Type

Quantity   Bullet Type Color Code

Non-Standard Ammunition tin and crate marking - Russian ammunition data

CASE TYPE MARKINGS

Mark	Meaning
ГЖ	Bimetallic case (gilding metal clad steel)
ГЛ	Brass case
ГС	Steel case

CARTRIDGE MFG FACTORY CODES

Code	Location
3	Ulyanovsk
17	Barnaul
38	Yuryuzan
60	Frunze (now Bishkek)
188	Novosibirsk
270	Voroshilovgrad (now Luhansk)
304	Lugansk
539	Tula
711	Klimovsk
T	Tula

Non-Standard Ammunition tin and crate marking - Russian ammunition data

BULLET TYPE MARKINGS

Mark	Meaning
Б Б-30 Б-32 БП	Armor-piercing
Б3	Armor-piercing incendiary
Б3Т Б3Т-44	Armor-piercing incendiary tracer
БС БС-40 БС-41	Armor-piercing with special core of tungsten carbide instead of carbon steel
БСТ	Armor-piercing with tungsten carbide core with added tracer
БТ	Armor-piercing tracer
Д	Heavy (long-range) with lead core instead of carbon steel
З ЗП	Incendiary
Л	Lightweight bullet
ЛПС	Light ball bullet with mild steel core
МДЗ	High explosive incendiary
П П-41	Spotting / ranging
ПЗ	Incendiary spotting / ranging
ПП	Enhanced penetration
ПС	Spotting / ranging with mild steel core
ПТ	Spotting / ranging tracer
СНБ	Armor-piercing sniper
Т Т-30 Т-45 Т-46	Tracer
57-У-322 57-У-323	Cartridge with higher powder charge
57-У-423	High-pressure cartridge
57-Х-322 57-Х-323 57-Х-340	Blank cartridge
57-НЕ-УЧ	Training cartridge
7Н1	Sniper bullet

BULLET TYPE COLOR CODES (Ammunition up to 14.5mm)

Color	Meaning
No color	Ball
White tip	Reference Ball
Silver tip	Light ball with steel core
Yellow tip	Heavy ball, or ball with torpedo base (on 7.62x54R)
Blue tip + white band	Short range ball 14.5x114 (only Hungarian and Czech)
Green tip + white band	Short range, tracer, (only Czech designation, only found on 7.62x39 with round nose)
Green tip	Tracer
Green tip & head-stamp or entire cartridge green	Subsonic ammunition for silencer-weapons
Red tip	Spotting charge, incendiary
Red tip + white band	Short range tracer ball 14.5x114 (only Hungarian designation)
Entire bullet red	High explosive bullet (7.62x54R after 1945)
Entire bullet red	High explosive bullet (on 12.7 and 14.5mm)
Magenta tip + red band	Armor piercing incendiary tracer
Black tip + red band	Armor piercing incendiary
Black tip + red shell	Armor piercing incendiary with tungsten carbide core
Black tip + yellow band	Armor piercing incendiary Phosphorus 12.7
Black tip	Armor piercing

** The bullet tip color codes in the table above will be the same color codes on the tins or crates, but they will be color stripes on the packaging.

Example:

<u>CARTRIDGE</u>
Black Tip + Red Band

<u>TIN or CRATE</u>
Black Stripe + Red Stripe

Appendix E - Non-Standard Weapon Identification Markings

General Identification Markings

There are various identification markings found on non-standard weapons. Typically the markings will provide some or all of the following information:
- factory name or stamp (proof mark)
- caliber & serial number
- selector lever markings/symbols
- rear sight mark/symbol

NOTE: Data tables are not all inclusive, but they cover the more common weapon manufacturers.

Selector Lever Markings on Kalashnikov Rifles

Upper/ Safe Symbol	Mid/ Full-Auto Symbol	Lower/ Semi-Auto Symbol	Country
	Д	1	Albania
	L	Ц	Albania
	AB	ЕД	Bulgaria
	L	Ц	China
	进	单	China
	30	1	Czechoslovakia
	آلي	فردي	Egypt
	D	E	Egypt
	D	E	East Germany
	∞	1	Hungary
أ	ص	م	Iraq
	련	단	North Korea
	C	P	Poland
	Z	O	Poland
S	A	R	Romania
S	FA	FF	Romania
	1	3	Romania
	ЛР	ОГОНЬ	Russia
	АВ	ОД	Russia
U	R	Ј	Yugo/Serbia

Rear Sight Marks on Kalashnikov Rifles

Symbol	Country
D	Albania
П	Bulgaria
D	China
N	East Germany
A	Hungary
Ⅱ	North Korea
S	Poland
P	Romania
П	Russia
O	Yugo/Serbia

Non-Standard Weapon Identification Markings

Factory Stamps and Countries of Manufacture

The table of symbols below are factory stamps (proof marks) for non-standard weapons. The symbols will identify the country of manufacture of the weapon. *NOTE: This is not an all inclusive list, but it covers the more common weapon manufacturers.*

(10) Bulgaria	(21) Bulgaria	(25) Bulgaria	China
(386) China	(36) China	(66) China	China
Egypt	East Germany	(3) East Germany	(K3) East Germany
East Germany	(06) East Germany	Iraq	Iraq
(star) North Korea	(star) North Korea	(11) Poland	Romania
Russia	Russia	Russia	Russia
Russia	Russia	Russia	Russia
Yugoslavia/Serbia	M.70.AB2 Yugoslavia/Serbia	ZASTAVA-KRAGUJEVAC Yugoslavia/Serbia	

Appendix F - Non-standard weapons theory overview

There are three key concepts to understand when manipulating non-standard weapons. These simple and logical concepts are:

1. CYCLE OF OPERATIONS
2. OPERATING SYSTEMS
3. LOCKING SYSTEMS

Firearm design trends are shared across region, manufacturer and class of weapon and are relatively obvious to recognize.

Keep in mind that firearms are essentially simple machines that harness the energy created by the fired cartridge to operate the system.

CYCLE OF OPERATIONS (COO)

The cycle of operations is a crucial basis for understanding how the weapon operates and for function/malfunction diagnosis. Each specific malfunction will correspond to a specific step or sometimes two in the COO. A failure in the system at a certain point, will by default, cause a failure of omission of all subsequent steps. (example – a failure to properly extract will manifest as a failure to eject.)

The COO will vary based on the type of operating and locking systems. Once the operating and locking systems of the weapon are known, the COO is logical.

The examples below all start from a standard reference point: the weapon is loaded, charged, placed on fire and the trigger is pulled.

'Cycle of Operations' Examples:

CLOSED BOLT	OPEN BOLT	BLOWBACK	BLOWBACK
Gas operated; roller locked delayed blowback; Browning recoil operating M2, MP5 and M1919 machine guns	Gas operated; MAG 58/M240 and M249 machine guns	(Pistol)	(Submachine Gun/Open Bolt)
FIRE 01	FEED 01	FIRE 01	FEED 01
UNLOCK 02	CHAMBER 02	~~UNLOCK~~	CHAMBER 02
EXTRACT 03	LOCK 03	EXTRACT 02	~~LOCK~~
EJECT 04	FIRE 04	EJECT 03	FIRE 03
COCK 05	UNLOCK 05	COCK 04	~~UNLOCK~~
FEED 06	EXTRACT 06 *	FEED 05	EXTRACT 04
CHAMBER 07	EJECT 07	CHAMBER 06	EJECT 05
LOCK 08	COCK 08	~~LOCK~~	COCK 06

*PKM will de-link at the same time

Non-standard weapons theory overview *(continued ...)*

⚙ ## OPERATING SYSTEMS

1. **Direct Impingement**- a type of gas operation that directs gas from a fired cartridge directly to the bolt carrier or slide assembly to cycle the action. (AR-15/M4 variants)

2. **Long-stroke piston system**- the piston is mechanically fixed to the bolt group and moves through the entire operating cycle. (AK variants)

3. **Short-stroke piston system (tappet system)**- the piston moves separately from the bolt group. It may directly push the bolt group parts as n the M1 carbine or operate through a connecting rod. (HK 416, AR180, POF, LWRC, FN FAL)

4. **Blowback**- the system of operation for self-loading firearms that obtains energy from the motion of the cartridge case as it is pushed to the rear by expanding gases created by the ignition of the propellant charge. (STEN, Makarov, M3 Grease Gun)

5. **Short recoil action**- the barrel and slide recoil only a short distance before they unlock and separate. The barrel stops quickly, and the slide continues rearward compressing the recoil spring and performing extraction, ejection and finally feeding a fresh round from the magazine in the counter recoil phase. During the last portion of its forward travel, the slide locks into the barrel and pushes the barrel back into battery. *(This is found in most handguns chambered for 9x19mm Parabellum or greater caliber. Smaller calibers, 9x18mm Makarov and below, generally use the blowback method of operation due to lower chamber pressure and associated simplicity of design.)

6. **Roller-locked, delayed-blowback**- when the bolt is closed, the rollers carried in the bolt are wedged into the receiver recesses. On firing, the rollers must be forced out of the recesses at great mechanical disadvantage, delaying the opening of the bolt, even with full power 7.62mm NATO (.308 Winchester) rifle cartridges used in the G3/HK 91 (G3, HK 91, HK 93, HK 53, MP5 variants)

7. **Inertia operated systems**- the bolt body is separated from the locked bolt body to remain stationary while the recoiling gun and locked bolt head moves rearward. This movement compresses the spring between the bolt head and bolt body, storing the energy required to cycle the action. Benelli shotguns.

Non-standard weapons theory overview *(continued ...)*

🔒 LOCKING SYSTEMS

1. **None** - all blowback pistols and some submachine guns – (STEN, UZI, M3 Grease Gun, Makarov, and CZ 82)

2. **Roller** - (HK variants, MG3, MG34, MG 42 and CZ 52)

3. **Rotating bolt** - (AK, Stoner, M60, and M249)

4. **Tilting bolt** - (SKS, FN FAL and MAG 58/M240)

5. **Tilting barrel** - (Tokarev TT33, Sig variants, M1911 variants and Glock variants)

6. **Rotating barrel** - (MAB P15, Colt All American 2000, and Beretta 8000)

7. **Locking flaps** - (RPD, DP/DPM and DShK)

8. **Falling locking block** - (P38, M9, and VZ58)

Function check
Checking the mechanical function of a weapon by replicating, without ammunition, the firing modes from the lowest rate of fire (SAFE if applicable) to the highest in a progressive sequence (not by selector location). The parts checked are the safety/safeties, sear and disconnector.

M4A1
1. Ensure the rifle is clear
2. Charge and place the weapon on SAFE
3. Attempt to fire (weapons should not FIRE, safety is functioning)
4. Place the weapon on SEMI, pull the trigger and hold it to the rear (hammer should fall, trigger/sear functioning)
5. Maintain the trigger to the rear and cycle the bolt
6. Release the trigger and listen for a metallic click (disconnector functioning)
7. Pull the trigger again and the hammer should fall
8. Charge the weapon and place on AUTO
9. Pull the trigger and hold it to the rear then cycle the bolt more than once
10. Release the trigger and pull it again, nothing should happen (auto sear is functioning)
11. Charge the weapon then pull the trigger again and the hammer should fall
12. Function check complete

Significant visual indicators
- Any checked, knurled or serrated surface
- Any movable lever or switch
- Pins with gripping surfaces
- Index marks (two lines that need to be aligned to disassembled (CZ 75)
- Recoil spring with ends of different diameters

www.ingramcontent.com/pod-product-compliance
Lightning Source LLC
Chambersburg PA
CBHW061056090426
42742CB00002B/60